Generative AI: From Buzzword to Business Value

Part 1: Unveiling the Power of Generative AI

Chapter 1: Demystifying Generative AI: Beyond the Hype

This chapter dives into the world of generative AI, separating the hype from the reality. We'll explore its historical roots within the broader field of Artificial Intelligence (AI), unpack the core concepts that make it tick, and showcase the transformative impact it's havingacross various industries.

1.1 A Historical Perspective: From Early AI to Generative Models

The dream of intelligent machines has captivated humanity for centuries. Early AI research, dating back to the 1950s, focused on symbolic approaches, attempting to encode knowledge and reasoning into rule-based systems. However, these systems struggled with the complexity of the real world.

The tides began to turn in the late 20th century with the emergenceof machine learning. This approach eschewed explicit programming,instead relying on algorithms that learn from data. This shift paved the way for the rise of deep learning in the early 2010s. Deep learning utilizes artificial neural networks, loosely inspired by the structure and function of the human brain, to process informationand identify patterns in vast amounts of data.

Generative AI is a subfield of deep learning that focuses on creating new data, be it text, images, music, or even scientific models. Unlike traditional AI that analyzes existing data, generative models learn theunderlying patterns and relationships within that data and use them to produce entirely new and original content. This ability to create opens up a wealth of possibilities across various fields.

1.2 Core Concepts: Understanding Generative

Models and TheirWorkings

While the specific details can get technical, understanding the core concepts behind generative models is crucial. Here's a breakdown ofsome key ideas:

- **Generative Models as Black Boxes:** Imagine a black box with data going in and new, creative content coming out. This is a simplified view of a generative model. It's trained on a massive dataset, learning the intricate relationships between differentelements within that data. Once trained, the model can then generate new outputs that resemble the training data but arenot simply copies.

- **Types of Generative Models:** There are different architectures for generative models, each with its strengths and weaknesses.Some popular examples include:

  - **Generative Adversarial Networks (GANs):** Imagine two AImodels pitted against each other. One, the generator, tries to create realistic data, while the other, the discriminator, tries to distinguish the generated data fromreal data. This constant competition leads to the generator improving its ability to produce realistic outputs.

- Variational Autoencoders (VAEs): These models encode the input data into a compressed representation and then learn to decode it back into a new, but similar, output.

VAEs are particularly useful for tasks like dimensionalityreduction and anomaly detection.

1.3 Applications Landscape: Exploring Generative AI's Impact AcrossIndustries

Generative AI is no longer a futuristic concept; it's activelytransforming industries. Here are some examples:

- **Media and Entertainment:** Generative AI is revolutionizing content creation. It can be used to generate realistic-looking images for movies and games, personalize music recommendations, or even create scripts for marketing campaigns.

- **Product Design and Development:**

  Imagine using AI to generate new product

  ideas or optimize existing designs.

  Generative models can analyze design

  trends and customerpreferences to

  suggest novel and innovative options.

- **Drug Discovery and Materials Science:**

  The ability to create new molecules with

  specific properties is a game-changer in

these fields. Generative AI can accelerate the development ofnew drugs and materials with desired functionalities.

This is just a glimpse into the vast potential of generative AI. The following sections will delve deeper into specific applications andexplore the challenges and considerations businesses need to address when implementing this powerful technology.

Chapter 2: The Inner Workings of Generative AI: A Technical Deep

2.1 Generative Model Architectures: Unveiling the Mechanisms

We touched upon different generative model architectures inChapter 1. Now, let's delve deeper into some popular ones:

- **Generative Adversarial Networks (GANs):** As mentioned earlier, GANs involve two neural networks locked in an adversarial battle. The **generator** network takes random noise as input and tries to create data that resembles the training data. The **discriminator** network, trained on real data, acts as agatekeeper, aiming to distinguish between real and generated data. Through this ongoing competition, the generator learns to produce increasingly realistic outputs that can fool the discriminator.

- **Variational Autoencoders (VAEs):** VAEs have two main components: an **encoder** and a **decoder**. The encoder takes input data and compresses it into a latent space, a lower-dimensional representation capturing the essence of the data.

The decoder then attempts to reconstruct the original data from this latent representation. However, during reconstruction, the decoder injects some randomness, leading to the generation of new data points similar to, but not identical to, the training data. VAEs are valuable for dimensionality reduction and anomaly detection, as data pointsthat fall outside the expected range in the latent space might be considered anomalies.

- **Autoregressive Models:** These models generate data one pieceat a time, like predicting the next word in a sentence. They are trained on a massive dataset, learning the probability of each element appearing based on the preceding elements. This allows them to generate sequential data, such as text, music, oreven code.

2.2 Training Generative Models: Data Preparation, OptimizationTechniques, and Challenges

Training generative models is no small feat. Here are some crucialaspects to consider:

- **Data Preparation:** Generative models are data-hungry. The quality and quantity of training data significantly impact the quality of the generated outputs. Data needs to be cleaned, pre-processed, and potentially augmented to ensure the modellearns the right patterns.

- **Optimization Techniques:** Training a generative model involvesfinding the optimal parameters for the underlying neural networks. Techniques like gradient descent and its variants areused to guide the model towards generating realistic outputs. However, these techniques can get stuck in local minima, generating subpar results.

- **Challenges:** Training generative models presents severalchallenges. These include:

  - **Mode Collapse:** The model might get stuck in a rut, generating the same type of output repeatedly instead of exploring the diverse possibilities within the data.

  - **Training Instability:** The adversarial nature of GANs canlead to training instability, where the generator and discriminator get locked in a loop, neither makingprogress.

- ○ **Computational Cost:** Training generative models, especially complex architectures, requires significant computational resources and can be time-consuming.

2.3 Evaluation Metrics: Assessing the Quality and Performance ofGenerated Content

Evaluating the quality of generated content is crucial. Here are somecommon metrics used:

- **Human Evaluation:** Subjective human evaluation remains the gold standard for tasks like image or text quality assessment.

Humans can judge the realism, coherence, and creativity of thegenerated content. However, this approach can be expensive and time-consuming.

- **Inception Score:** This metric leverages a pre-trained image classification model to assess the quality of generated images.

It measures how well the model classifies the generated imagesand how diverse the generated outputs are.

- **Frechet Inception Distance (FID):** Similar to the Inception Score, FID uses a pre-trained model to compare the distributionof features between real and generated data. A lower FID indicates a closer match between the two distributions, suggesting higher quality generated content.

These are just a few of the considerations for training and evaluatinggenerative models. As the field evolves, new techniques and metricsare constantly being developed to improve the training process and ensure the quality of generated

content.

Chapter 3: Mastering the Art of Text Generation

The ability to generate human-quality text is revolutionizing communication and content creation. This chapter explores the diverse applications of text-based generative AI and the challengesthat need to be addressed.

3.1 From Chatbots to Content Creation: Applications of TextGenerative AI

Text generation is one of the most mature areas of generative AI.Here are some exciting ways it's being used:

- **Chatbots and Virtual Assistants:** Generative

AI powers chatbots that can hold natural conversations, answer questions, and provide customer support. These chatbots canpersonalize interactions and learn from each other, leading tomore engaging and helpful experiences.

- **Content Marketing and Advertising:** Imagine creating personalized marketing copy, product descriptions, or social media posts tailored to specific audiences. Generative AI can automate content creation at scale while maintaining aconsistent brand voice.

- **Journalism and News Reporting:** AI can assist journalists by generating reports on financial data or summarizing large datasets. However, ethical considerations regarding bias andthe potential for misinformation need to be carefully addressed.

- **Creative Writing and Education:** Generative AI can be a powerful tool for creative exploration. It can inspire new ideas,help overcome writer's block, or even co-write poems, scripts, or even song lyrics. In education, it can be used to personalize learning materials or create interactive narratives.

3.2 Exploring Different Text Formats: News Articles, Poetry, CodeGeneration

The capabilities of text-based generative AI extend beyond simplesentences. Here are some fascinating applications:

- **News Article Summarization and Generation:** Imagine automatically generating summaries of news articles or even creating personalized news feeds based on reader preferences. Generative AI can process vast amounts of information and extract key points for concise and informative summaries.

- **Poetry and Creative Text Formats:** While some may scoff at theidea of AI-generated poetry, these models can be surprisingly creative. They can mimic existing styles or even generate new and unexpected forms of expression.

- **Code Generation:** Programmers can leverage generative AI toautomate repetitive coding tasks or even generate code snippets based on natural language descriptions. This can significantly improve developer productivity.

3.3 Challenges and Considerations: Bias, Factuality, andMaintaining Control

Despite its potential, text generation with AI comes with challenges:

- **Bias:** Text generative models are trained on massive amountsof data, which can reflect societal biases. This can lead to outputs that are discriminatory or offensive. Mitigating bias requires careful data selection and model design.

- **Factuality and Truth Detection:** AI-generated text can be highlybelievable, even if it's factually incorrect. It's crucial to implement fact-checking mechanisms and ensure transparencyabout the source of generated content.

- **Maintaining Control:** When using AI for creative writing, it'simportant to strike a balance between letting the model contribute and maintaining control over

the final output. Finding the right balance

allows human creativity to flourish

alongside the power of AI.

By acknowledging these challenges and

implementing responsibledevelopment

practices, text-based generative AI holds

immense potential for communication, content

creation, and artistic expression.

Chapter 4: Shaping the Visual World: Generative AI for Image andVideo Creation

The world of visual media is undergoing a revolution with the adventof generative AI. This chapter dives into the exciting world of image and video generation, exploring its potential and the ethical considerations that come with it.

4.1 From Photorealistic Images to Style Transfer: Exploring ImageGeneration Techniques

Generative AI is pushing the boundaries of image creation. Let'sdelve into some of the techniques used to create stunning and realistic visuals:

- **Generative Adversarial Networks (GANs):** As explored in Chapter 2, GANs play a starring role in image generation. A GAN pitts two neural networks against each other, with the generator creating images and the discriminator trying to distinguish real from generated ones. This competition drives the generator to produce increasingly realistic and high-fidelityimages.

- **Variational Autoencoders (VAEs):** VAEs offer another approach. They compress an image into a latent space, a lower-dimensional representation capturing its essence. The decoder then reconstructs the image from this latent space. By introducing randomness during reconstruction, VAEs can generate new images that share similarities with the training data but also exhibit creative variations.

- **Style Transfer:** Imagine applying the artistic style of a famous painter to a photograph. Generative AI models can achieve thisfeat by separating the content of an image (what the image depicts) from its style (the artistic elements like brushstrokes orcolor palettes). This allows for creative exploration and the generation of unique visuals.

4.2 Generative Video: Creating Realistic and Artistic Video Content

Moving beyond static images, generative AI is making waves in videocreation as well:

- **Generating Realistic Videos:** Similar to image generation techniques, GANs and other models can be used to create realistic videos. This opens doors for applications like creatingspecial effects for movies or generating personalized video content in marketing campaigns.

- **Video Editing and Style Transfer:** Imagine automatically generating different edits of a video or applying artistic styles to existing video footage. Generative AI can streamline video editing workflows and offer creative possibilities for filmmakersand content creators.

- **Video Summarization:** Conveying the key

points of a long videocan be time-consuming.

Generative AI models can automatically

summarize video content, creating shorter

clips that capture the essence of the original

video.

4.3 Ethical Considerations: Addressing Bias and Potential Misuse inImage/Video Generation

The power of image and video generation

comes with ethicalconsiderations:

- **Bias:** Generative models trained on biased data can perpetuate those biases in the images and videos they create. It's crucial to ensure diverse datasets and monitor outputs for potential bias.

- **Deepfakes and Misinformation:** The ability to create realistic videos of people saying or doing things they never did poses a significant threat. Mitigating the spread of misinformation created with deepfakes requires technological solutions and heightened media literacy.

- **Privacy Concerns:** The ability to manipulate or generate images/videos of people raises privacy concerns. Regulations and responsible development practices are essential to protectindividual privacy.

By acknowledging these challenges and working towards solutions,generative AI can be a powerful tool for visual storytelling, creativeexpression, and content creation, all while ensuring ethical and responsible use

Generative AI: From Buzzword to Business Value

Generative AI, once a buzzword in tech circles, has evolved into a transformative force across industries. Its rapid development has moved beyond theoretical discussions to real-world applications that are redefining how businesses operate, create, and engage with customers. The technology, driven by large language models (LLMs), deep learning, and neural networks, has enabled advancements in natural language processing (NLP), computer vision, and audio generation, unlocking new possibilities for automation, creativity, and personalization. This chapter delves into how generative AI has made its way from a conceptual tool to a critical business asset, exploring its current applications, the challenges businesses face, and the path forward.

The Rise of Generative AI: A Technological Evolution

Generative AI's evolution has been largely shaped by breakthroughs in deep learning. In its earliest stages, AI was mainly seen in narrow, task-specific applications, such as rule-based expert systems or traditional machine learning techniques that required significant human intervention to produce useful outputs. However, with the introduction of more sophisticated architectures like Generative Adversarial Networks (GANs), Variational Autoencoders (VAEs), and transformers, the scope of AI expanded dramatically. The pivotal moment came with the development of large-scale unsupervised models, most notably GPT-3 and GPT-4, which demonstrated the ability to generate human-like text based on vast datasets of text from the internet. These models were capable not just of following instructions, but of creating novel text, art, code, and even music— abilities that were previously thought to be far beyond the reach of artificial intelligence.

While generative AI has existed in some form for years, the last few years have seen an explosion in both the capability and the use cases of the technology. The growth of open-source tools, the increasing availability of massive computational resources, and the accumulation of diverse and high-quality training data have all contributed to the current generative AI boom. Its potential is evident, as more and more companies are exploring and adopting generative AI technologies to drive business value.

Generative AI in Business: Transforming Operations and Strategy

The applications of generative AI in business are broad, ranging from automating tedious tasks to revolutionizing the customer experience. These applications are deeply intertwined with the principles of innovation and cost-efficiency. With its ability to mimic, create, and enhance human-like creativity, generative AI is enabling new business models that were previously unimaginable.

Automation of Content Creation

In the realm of marketing, one of the most impactful uses of generative AI is in automating content creation. With AI systems like GPT-4, companies are now able to generate marketing copy, blog posts, product descriptions, and even social media content at a fraction of the time it would take human writers. Generative AI is capable of not only creating content but also optimizing it based on past performance data, enhancing SEO, and tailoring it to specific customer demographics. This reduces the overhead for content teams and accelerates the process of scaling content production.

For instance, ecommerce businesses can automate product descriptions in multiple languages, write customer-facing emails, and generate targeted advertisements, all while maintaining a consistent tone and branding. This ability to scale content generation while maintaining relevance is crucial for industries where time-to-market is a critical factor in success.

Personalization and Customer Experience

Generative AI is also playing a key role in personalizing the customer experience. In industries like retail, banking, and healthcare, personalization is paramount. Generative models can analyze vast amounts of data—whether it's customer behavior, purchase history, or even sentiment analysis from social media—and create personalized recommendations or communications that are both relevant and timely.

In the fashion industry, AI-driven design tools allow companies to create personalized clothing suggestions based on customers' past choices, body types, and even preferred fabrics. For example, brands like Stitch Fix have incorporated AI to generate clothing recommendations for their customers, with models suggesting pieces that the customer may not have considered themselves. Similarly, in the financial sector, generative AI is used to create personalized investment strategies or financial advice, helping financial advisors create tailored portfolios for individual clients.

Beyond personalization of products, AI can generate personalized content experiences, such as custom news feeds, tailored email campaigns, or specialized educational resources, enhancing engagement and improving conversion rates.

The potential for generative AI in product development and innovation is profound. In industries such as pharmaceuticals, automotive, and consumer electronics, AI models are being used to generate novel ideas for new products or services. For example, generative AI models are being used to design drugs in the pharmaceutical industry. These models analyze existing molecular data and generate new compounds that could be potential treatments for diseases, significantly speeding up the process of drug discovery.

In the automotive industry, generative AI has been applied to design car parts and optimize the layout of vehicles. Using generative design algorithms, companies like General Motors and Boeing have reduced manufacturing costs by optimizing the material usage and improving part strength without compromising performance. These AI-driven designs are not only more efficient but also allow companies to push the boundaries of innovation in ways that were previously too costly or time-consuming.

Moreover, generative AI enables faster iteration cycles in product design. Instead of requiring human engineers to manually test thousands of variations, AI can simulate and test a multitude of designs in parallel, narrowing down the most optimal options quickly.

Enhancing Creativity and Media Production

Generative AI has also made significant inroads into the creative industries, from art and music to filmmaking and video games. In music, for instance, AI models can generate entirely new pieces of music based on various styles, genres, or even specific artists. Artists and producers use these tools to brainstorm new ideas, experiment with different musical compositions, and speed up the creation of background scores and soundtracks.

In visual arts, AI models like DALL-E and Artbreeder can generate original artwork based on textual prompts, allowing designers and artists to use AI-generated images as inspiration or even as part of their creative process. AI-generated art is becoming an increasingly popular tool in commercial advertising, where brands use unique AI-generated visuals to capture the attention of their audience.

AI is also revolutionizing film production, particularly in animation and visual effects. Studios use generative AI to speed up the animation process, create realistic digital doubles of actors, and generate visual effects that would be prohibitively expensive using traditional methods.

AI-Powered Chatbots and Virtual Assistants

Another significant application of generative AI is in customer support through the use of intelligent chatbots and virtual assistants. AI-driven chatbots like

OpenAI's ChatGPT, and conversational agents integrated into customer service platforms, are becoming increasingly sophisticated in handling complex customer queries. These systems are capable of understanding context, interpreting nuanced language, and generating human-like responses, making them more effective than traditional rule-based chatbots.

Businesses are employing these AI systems to handle a large volume of customer inquiries, improving response times and reducing operational costs. Chatbots can be integrated into websites, mobile apps, and social media platforms to assist customers 24/7, providing a personalized and efficient experience.

Beyond simple FAQ responses, these systems can assist in troubleshooting, providing product recommendations, or even guiding users through a complex service process.

The latest iterations of generative AI-powered assistants also integrate multimodal capabilities—combining text, voice, and even visual inputs. This allows them to offer more personalized and context-aware support, creating a seamless experience for customers across various channels.

Challenges and Ethical Considerations

While generative AI offers immense potential, its widespread adoption comes with several challenges and ethical considerations. One of the most pressing issues is the potential for bias in AI models. Because generative AI systems are trained on vast datasets scraped from the internet, they may inadvertently reinforce biases related to gender, race, and other social constructs. For example, a generative model trained on internet data could perpetuate harmful stereotypes, which could have serious consequences in applications like hiring, law enforcement, and healthcare.

Moreover, the use of generative AI raises questions about intellectual property and originality. If an AI model creates a piece of music, artwork, or writing, who owns the rights to that work? Is it the developer of the AI, the business using it, or the AI itself? These legal uncertainties are compounded by concerns about plagiarism and the authenticity of AI-generated content. While generative AI is capable of producing new and unique content, the fact that its output is based on prior training data raises questions about the true creativity of these models.

Additionally, businesses need to ensure transparency and accountability when deploying AI systems. The "black box" nature of many generative models makes it difficult to understand how decisions are made or why a particular output is generated. This lack of interpretability is a concern for industries like healthcare and finance, where decisions made by AI can have significant real-world consequences.

Companies must invest in explainability and ensure that their AI systems are auditable and ethically sound.

Finally, the use of generative AI presents significant cybersecurity risks. As generative models become more powerful, they can be used to create deepfakes, misinformation, and other malicious content. Businesses and governments will need to implement robust security measures to detect and mitigate the risks associated with AI-generated disinformation, which could have far-reaching consequences for society.

The Future of Generative AI in Business

As generative AI continues to mature, its impact on business will only grow. Future advancements may include even more sophisticated models capable of producing multimedia content, including high-quality video generation and real-time audio synthesis. These capabilities will enable new forms of customer interaction and creative expression, opening up further opportunities for personalization, entertainment, and digital transformation.

Furthermore, as AI models become more efficient, their integration into day-to-day business operations will become increasingly seamless. We may see AI systems that not only generate content but also make strategic decisions, analyze vast datasets in real time, and predict market trends with unprecedented accuracy. Generative AI will play a key role in shaping business strategies, driving efficiency, and fostering innovation.

The ongoing evolution of generative AI suggests that businesses must continue to adapt, innovate, and stay ahead of the curve in this fast-moving field. By leveraging the capabilities of generative AI, businesses can gain a competitive edge, enhance customer experiences, and unlock new sources of value, making AI a core driver of business transformation in the years to come.

Business Process Automation and Generative AI

Generative AI is playing an increasingly central role in transforming business processes by automating tasks that were once labor-intensive and prone to human error. The rise of AI-powered tools in business operations is enhancing efficiency and freeing up human resources for more strategic, value-added tasks. From document generation to real-time decision-making, AI is changing how companies operate internally and interact with customers.

In many organizations, administrative tasks such as data entry, scheduling, and document management were traditionally handled manually. Generative AI can automate these processes, reducing time spent on routine work and eliminating errors. For instance,

AI systems can automatically generate reports based on real-time data, draft emails, or even handle basic customer service inquiries, which traditionally required a significant amount of human labor.

Generative AI is also enhancing decision-making processes within businesses. By leveraging large datasets and predictive models, businesses can gain actionable insights that would otherwise be impossible to uncover. For example, in the field of finance, AI can automatically analyze market trends, generate predictions about future stock movements, and offer insights that help businesses make informed decisions quickly.

One area where generative AI is particularly useful is customer service. AI-driven chatbots and virtual assistants are now capable of handling a wide variety of customer inquiries, ranging from basic troubleshooting to complex problem resolution. These systems can generate responses dynamically based on a customer's unique needs and historical interactions, providing a more personalized and efficient customer experience.

Generative AI in Marketing and Customer Personalization

Generative AI is revolutionizing marketing by enabling businesses to create highly personalized customer experiences at scale. The power of generative AI lies in its ability to process vast amounts of data and generate tailored content that resonates with individual consumers. This allows businesses to target customers more precisely, leading to higher conversion rates and stronger customer loyalty.

In marketing, generative AI is often used to create personalized ad copy, email campaigns, and social media content. By analyzing customer behavior, preferences, and purchase history, AI can generate marketing materials that speak directly to the individual's interests. For example, an AI model might generate an email campaign offering products that are highly likely to appeal to a specific customer based on their previous interactions with the brand.

AI-powered tools can also automate the generation of content for websites, blogs, and social media platforms, making it easier for businesses to maintain an active online presence. These tools can generate posts, articles, and product descriptions that are relevant to specific customer segments, driving engagement and increasing brand awareness.

Another significant area where generative AI is having an impact is in the creation of dynamic pricing models. By analyzing consumer behavior, market trends, and competitor pricing, AI can automatically generate optimized pricing strategies that maximize revenue and improve competitiveness. This enables businesses to offer personalized pricing to customers based on their likelihood to purchase, their loyalty to the brand, and other factors.

AI-Driven Innovation in Product Development

Generative AI is playing an increasingly important role in product development, from ideation to prototyping and market testing. Traditionally, product development involved extensive human brainstorming, design, and testing. With the introduction of generative AI, this process is becoming faster, more efficient, and more data-driven.

AI can now generate new product ideas based on consumer trends, competitive analysis, and market research. By processing large datasets, generative AI can identify gaps in the market and suggest innovative product features that meet customer needs. In industries like fashion or consumer electronics, AI systems can generate designs or prototypes based on current trends and consumer feedback, accelerating the time to market for new products.

Beyond product design, AI is also being used to test and refine products before they are released to the market. Generative AI can simulate user experiences, predict how a product will perform under different conditions, and even analyze customer feedback to recommend improvements. This allows companies to create better products that are more likely to succeed in the market, reducing the risk of failure and ensuring a more efficient development process.

The Role of Generative AI in Supply Chain Optimization

Generative AI is having a transformative effect on supply chain management by optimizing everything from inventory control to demand forecasting and logistics. By harnessing the power of AI, businesses can streamline their supply chain operations, reduce costs, and improve customer satisfaction.

AI-driven systems can analyze historical sales data, seasonal trends, and external factors such as weather or economic conditions to generate accurate demand forecasts. This enables businesses to optimize their inventory levels, ensuring they have the right products on hand at the right time without overstocking or understocking.

Generative AI also plays a crucial role in logistics and route planning. By analyzing traffic patterns, fuel costs, and delivery schedules, AI can generate optimized routes for shipments, reducing fuel consumption and delivery times. This not only lowers costs but also enhances the overall efficiency of the supply chain, ensuring that products reach customers faster and more reliably.

In addition, AI can help businesses improve supplier relationships by analyzing supplier performance data and recommending adjustments to the supply chain. For example, if a particular supplier is consistently late with deliveries, AI can identify alternative suppliers or recommend process changes to mitigate delays, ensuring that businesses maintain a steady flow of products.

Ethical and Responsible Use of Generative AI in Business

As generative AI becomes more integrated into business operations, organizations must also consider the ethical implications of its use. From data privacy to bias in AI models, companies must navigate a complex landscape of challenges to ensure that their use of generative AI is responsible, fair, and transparent.

One of the key concerns around generative AI is the potential for bias in AI models. AI systems are trained on vast amounts of data, and if that data contains biases—whether in terms of gender, race, or socioeconomic status—those biases can be reflected in the outputs generated by the AI. For example, a generative AI system used in hiring or recruitment might produce biased recommendations if it is trained on biased historical data. To address this issue, businesses must prioritize diversity and fairness in the data they use to train AI models and implement safeguards to detect and correct biases in AI-generated outputs.

Another ethical concern is data privacy. With AI systems processing large volumes of personal data, it is essential that businesses take measures to protect customer privacy and comply with regulations such as GDPR. AI systems must be designed to ensure that customer data is handled securely and that personal information is not used inappropriately or shared without consent.

Finally, businesses must be transparent in how they use generative AI. This includes informing customers about the role AI plays in decision-making processes and providing mechanisms for customers to understand and challenge AI-generated outcomes. By being transparent about the capabilities and limitations of AI, businesses can build trust with their customers and ensure that AI is used in a way that benefits everyone.

Generative AI in Human Resources and Talent

Management

Generative AI is transforming the way organizations approach human resources and talent management, enabling smarter, data-driven decisions that improve hiring processes, employee engagement, and talent development. Traditionally, HR departments relied on time-consuming manual processes to recruit, train, and retain employees. Today, AI-driven tools are automating and optimizing many of these tasks, offering HR teams more precise insights and enabling them to make better-informed decisions.

One of the most impactful applications of generative AI in HR is recruitment. AI-powered systems can now analyze vast amounts of candidate data, from resumes to social media profiles, and generate highly targeted recommendations. By matching candidate profiles with job descriptions, AI can identify individuals who are best suited for particular roles based on a combination of experience, skills, personality, and cultural fit. In addition, AI tools can help eliminate unconscious bias in hiring by focusing on objective data rather than subjective factors, ensuring a more diverse and inclusive hiring process.

Beyond recruitment, generative AI is improving employee training and development. AI systems can personalize learning experiences for employees, recommending courses or resources based on an individual's job role, career goals, and learning preferences. Furthermore, AI-driven platforms can generate dynamic training content, such as personalized quizzes, simulations, and real-time feedback, allowing employees to learn more efficiently and effectively.

AI is also playing a significant role in employee engagement and retention. By analyzing employee feedback, sentiment data, and performance metrics, AI can generate insights that help HR departments identify potential issues before they become major problems. For example, AI can detect early signs of employee burnout or dissatisfaction and recommend proactive measures to improve morale and reduce turnover.

Generative AI in Finance and Risk Management

Generative AI is making waves in the finance industry by transforming how institutions manage risk, analyze financial data, and make investment decisions. AI-powered models are now able to generate accurate financial forecasts, optimize portfolios, and automate regulatory compliance, driving efficiency and improving decision-making at every level of the financial ecosystem.

One of the key applications of generative AI in finance is risk management. AI systems can process and analyze vast amounts of financial data in real time, identifying patterns and predicting potential risks with unparalleled accuracy. For example, AI can generate models to forecast market volatility, assess credit risk, or detect fraudulent activity. These models help financial institutions make more informed decisions, mitigate potential losses, and ensure compliance with regulatory requirements.

In portfolio management, generative AI is enabling the creation of more optimized investment strategies. By analyzing historical performance, market conditions, and economic factors, AI can generate personalized investment recommendations for clients, balancing risk and reward in ways that would be nearly impossible for human analysts to achieve. Additionally, AI can simulate various investment scenarios and predict how portfolios will perform under different market conditions, helping investors make better long-term decisions.

Another major benefit of AI in finance is its ability to automate tasks that were previously manual and time-consuming. For instance, AI can be used to automate the generation of financial reports, streamlining compliance with accounting standards and regulatory frameworks. By automating these tasks, financial institutions can focus more on strategic decision-making, while reducing operational costs and minimizing human error.

Generative AI in Healthcare: Transforming Diagnosis, Treatment, and Drug Discovery

The healthcare industry is one of the most promising sectors where generative AI is poised to make a significant impact. From revolutionizing patient care to accelerating drug discovery, AI has the potential to fundamentally change how healthcare providers deliver services and how researchers develop new therapies. The ability of generative AI to analyze vast amounts of medical data, generate personalized treatment plans, and optimize healthcare workflows is transforming the industry in ways that were once considered impossible.

One of the most exciting applications of generative AI in healthcare is in diagnostics. AI models can analyze medical images, patient records, and genetic data to generate highly accurate diagnoses for a wide range of conditions, from cancer to neurological disorders. By processing these complex datasets, generative AI can help healthcare providers identify patterns and make predictions that may be missed by human doctors. For example, AI-powered systems are already being used to generate radiology reports from medical images, identifying abnormalities with a level of precision that rivals or even exceeds that of human radiologists.

In personalized medicine, generative AI is enabling the creation of treatment plans tailored to individual patients. By analyzing genetic data, lifestyle factors, and medical histories, AI can generate personalized recommendations for drug therapies or lifestyle changes that are most likely to benefit the patient. This not only improves patient outcomes but also reduces the trial-and-error approach often associated with medical treatment, making healthcare more efficient and cost-effective.

In drug discovery, generative AI is accelerating the process of developing new therapies by generating novel molecular structures that could potentially lead to the development of new drugs. By using AI to simulate how different compounds will interact with specific targets in the body, researchers can identify promising drug candidates faster and at a fraction of the cost of traditional methods. AI is also being used to predict the side effects of drugs, making the development process safer and more effective.

Generative AI is also playing a crucial role in optimizing healthcare operations. From scheduling and resource allocation to patient triage, AI is automating routine tasks, improving operational efficiency, and freeing up healthcare professionals to focus on direct patient care. For example, AI-powered scheduling systems can generate optimal appointment times based on patient needs, available resources, and doctor schedules, reducing wait times and improving patient satisfaction.

Chapter 5: Pushing the Boundaries: Generative AI Beyond Text andImages

Generative AI's reach extends far beyond the realm of text and images. This chapter explores its applications in composing music, scientific discovery, and even pushing the boundaries of design. We'llalso delve into the exciting possibilities that lie ahead.

5.1 Generative Music and Audio: Composing New Pieces andAltering Existing Ones

The world of music is being reshaped by generative AI. Here aresome fascinating applications:

- **Music Composition:** Generative models can compose original pieces of music in various styles. Imagine an AI that can createmusic reminiscent of a famous composer or even generate entirely new musical genres.

- **Music Editing and Remixing:** AI can assist musicians by automatically generating remixes, creating variations on existing pieces, or personalizing music for individual listeners.

- **Sound Design and Audio Effects:** Generative models can createrealistic sound effects or even design soundscapes for movies, video games, or virtual reality experiences.

5.2 Scientific Applications: Drug Discovery, Material Science, andGenerative Design

The potential of generative AI extends beyond creative pursuits. It'stransforming scientific research in fascinating ways:

- **Drug Discovery:** The process of discovering new drugs is traditionally slow and expensive. Generative AI can acceleratethis process by designing new molecules with specific properties that could lead to lifesaving medications.

- **Material Science:** Similar to drug discovery, generative AI can be used to design new materials with desired properties, suchas stronger, lighter, or more efficient materials for various applications.

- **Generative Design:** Imagine using AI to design products or processes. Generative models can explore vast design spaces, suggesting innovative solutions that human designers mightmiss. This can optimize product design for functionality, aesthetics, or even manufacturability.

5.3 The Future Landscape: Emerging Applications and UnforeseenPossibilities

Generative AI is a rapidly evolving field, and new applications areconstantly emerging. Here's a glimpse into the future:

- **Personalized Experiences:** Generative AI can personalize experiences across various domains. Imagine educational materials that adapt to a student's learning style or travel experiences tailored to individual preferences.

- **Generative AI for Social Good:** AI-generated content can be used for social good, such as creating educational materials in underserved communities or personalizing healthcare interventions.

- **The Unforeseen:** As generative AI continues to develop, it's difficult to predict all its future applications. The possibilities are vast and constantly expanding,

with the potential torevolutionize

many aspects of our lives.

However, it's important to acknowledge that

alongside these excitingprospects, there are

challenges to consider. Ensuring responsible

development, addressing potential biases in AI

models, and navigating the ethical implications of

this powerful technology will becrucial as generative

AI shapes the future.

Part 3: Business Value of Generative AI

Chapter 6: Generative AI for Business Transformation

Generative AI is no longer a technology of the future; it's a practical tool with the potential to revolutionize businesses across all industries. This chapter explores how generative models can be usedto identify new opportunities, streamline processes, and drive innovation.

6.1 Identifying Business Opportunities: A Use Case Framework forGenerative AI

The possibilities with generative AI are vast, but it's crucial to identifyapplications that align with your specific business goals. Here's a framework to help you explore potential use cases:

- Content Creation and Marketing:

  - Generate personalized marketing copy, product descriptions, or social media posts tailored to specificaudience segments.
  - Create engaging video ads or product demos usinggenerative AI for video creation.

- Personalize customer email campaigns with targetedmessaging based on individual preferences.
- Product Development and Design:

  - Utilize generative design to explore vast design spacesand discover innovative product concepts.
  - Optimize product design for functionality, aesthetics, and manufacturability.
  - Generate realistic product mockups and prototypes foruser testing and feedback.
- Customer Service and Support:

- Develop chatbots powered by generative AI to provide24/7 customer support and answer frequently asked questions.

- Personalize customer service interactions by recommending relevant products or services based onpast behavior.

- Automate repetitive tasks within the customer service department, freeing up human agents for more complex inquiries.

- Research and Development:

  - Use generative AI to accelerate drug discovery bydesigning new molecules with desired properties.
  - Streamline material science research by generating newmaterials with specific functionalities.
  - Personalize healthcare interventions by analyzing patientdata and generating

tailored treatment plans.

These are just a few examples, and the potential applications of generative AI vary greatly depending on the industry. Here are someadditional considerations when identifying use cases:

- Data Availability: Generative models are data-driven. Ensureyou have access to high-quality, relevant data to train your models effectively.

- Technical Expertise: Implementing generative AI solutionsmight require specialized skills within your organization.

Evaluate your technical resources or consider partnering withAI experts.

- Return on Investment (ROI): Carefully assess the potential ROIof a generative AI project. Consider the costs associated with technology, data, and implementation compared to the expected benefits.

By considering these factors and following a structured approach, you can identify high-value use cases for generative AI that drive realbusiness transformation.

6.2 Business Process Optimization through Generative Models Beyond creating new opportunities, generative AI can also streamline existing business processes. Let's explore some ways:

- Automating Repetitive Tasks: Generative models can automate tasks that are currently performed manually by employees. This can free up valuable human resources for more strategic work.

- Data Analysis and Insights Generation: Generative AI can analyze vast amounts of data and identify patterns or trends that might be missed by humans. This can lead to improveddecision-making and increased efficiency.

- Personalized Customer Experiences: Generative AI can personalize customer experiences across all touchpoints. Thiscan lead to increased customer satisfaction and loyalty.

- Risk Management and Fraud Detection: Generative models canbe used to identify potential risks or fraudulent activity by analyzing data and predicting future trends.

Optimizing business processes with generative AI can lead to significant improvements in efficiency, productivity, and overall business performance.

However, it's important to remember that Alis not a silver bullet.

6.3 Balancing Human and Machine Intelligence

While generative AI can automate tasks and provide valuable insights, human expertise remains essential. Businesses should strivefor a balance between human and machine intelligence, leveraging the strengths of both.

For example, generative AI might generate initial product design concepts, but human designers would refine and finalize these concepts based on their creative vision and understanding of userneeds.

By adopting a human-centered approach to AI implementation, businesses can unlock the full potential of generative AI for processoptimization and overall business transformation.

Chapter 7: The Generative AI Revolution: Shaping the Future ofBusiness and Society

Generative AI is no longer a distant promise; it's actively reshapingindustries and impacting society as a whole. This chapter explores the potential future of generative AI, the societal implications it raises, and the importance of responsible development.

7.1 Forecasting the Future: The Potential Impact of Generative AIon Different Industries

The impact of generative AI will be felt across various industries.Here's a glimpse into the future:

- **Marketing and Advertising:** Imagine personalized marketing campaigns tailored to individual customers or AI-generated product recommendations that anticipate consumer needs. Generative AI can revolutionize how businesses connect with their audience.

- **Manufacturing and Design:** Generative models can optimizeproduct design for functionality, aesthetics, and even manufacturability. This can lead to more efficient productionprocesses, innovative product development, and potentially lower costs.

- **Healthcare and Medicine:** Generative AI is accelerating drugdiscovery and personalized medicine. It can assist in medicaldiagnosis, designing prosthetic limbs, or even personalizing treatment plans for individual patients.

- **Education and Training:** Imagine personalized learning materials that adapt to a student's learning style or AI-poweredtutors that provide real-time feedback. Generative AI has the potential to transform education and make it more engaging and effective.

These are just a few examples, and the potential applications of generative AI are constantly expanding. As the technology matures,we can expect to see its influence in nearly every area of our lives. However, alongside the benefits, there are societal implications to consider.

7.2 Societal Implications: Considering Ethical, Legal, and RegulatoryFrameworks

The power of generative AI comes with responsibilities. Here aresome key societal considerations:

- **Bias and Fairness:** Generative models trained on biased data can perpetuate those biases in their outputs. Developing fair and ethical AI models that represent diversity and avoid discrimination requires careful attention to data selection andmodel design.

- **Job displacement:** Automation driven by AI may lead to job displacement in certain sectors. Governments, businesses, and educational institutions need to work together to provide retraining opportunities and prepare the workforce for the future.

- **Deepfakes and Misinformation:** The ability to create realistic videos of people saying or doing things they never did poses athreat to trust and democracy. Regulatory frameworks and technological solutions are needed to

combat the spread ofmisinformation

created with deepfakes.

- **Privacy Concerns:** The ability to manipulate

  or generate images/videos of people raises

  privacy concerns. Regulations and responsible

  development practices are essential to

  protectindividual privacy.

Addressing these societal implications requires a

multi-pronged approach involving collaboration

between governments, businesses,and academia.

Ethical guidelines, legal frameworks, and

responsible development practices are crucial to

ensure that generative AI benefits society as a

whole.

7.3 The Responsible Development of Generative AI: EnsuringTransparency and Fairness

The future of generative AI hinges on responsible development. Hereare some key principles:

- **Transparency:** Understanding how generative models work andthe limitations of their outputs is crucial. Businesses and developers should be transparent about the use of AI andensure user awareness.

- **Fairness and Mitigating Bias:** As discussed earlier, mitigating bias in generative models requires diverse datasets and carefulmodel design. Ongoing monitoring and evaluation are essentialto ensure fairness and inclusivity.

- **Human oversight:** Generative AI should not replace humanjudgment, especially in critical decision-making processes. Human oversight and control over AI outputs are vital for responsible use.

- **Collaboration:** Developing and deploying generative AI effectively requires collaboration between technologists, ethicists, policymakers, and the public.

Open discussions andshared responsibility

are key to shaping the future of this

powerful technology.

By embracing these principles, we can ensure

that generative AI remains a force for good,

driving innovation, progress, and a more

equitable future.

Generative AI in Creative Industries: Redefining Art, Music, and Content Creation

Generative AI is profoundly reshaping the creative industries, offering new tools and capabilities that redefine the boundaries of art, music, literature, and digital content creation. By combining advanced machine learning models with the immense potential for creative expression, AI is empowering artists, musicians, writers, and designers to break free from traditional constraints and explore innovative possibilities that were previously unimaginable.

In the world of visual arts, generative AI tools like DALL·E and MidJourney have gained significant attention for their ability to create stunningly realistic images, surreal art pieces, and conceptual designs based on simple textual descriptions. These tools use deep learning models trained on vast datasets of visual content to generate original artwork, often with intricate detail and creativity that can rival human-made designs. This technology is being embraced by artists and designers as a way to augment their creative process, providing inspiration, generating draft compositions, and even collaborating with AI to produce entirely new forms of art.

Generative AI is not just transforming visual art; it is also making waves in music production. AI systems such as OpenAI's Jukedeck and Aiva are capable of composing original music in various genres, from classical to contemporary. These AI models are trained on large music datasets, learning patterns, structures, and harmonies that can be replicated or innovated upon to create new compositions. Musicians and composers are now using AI to assist with writing melodies, harmonies, and even lyrics. In some cases, AI can generate entire songs or soundtracks for films, video games, or advertisements, reducing production time and allowing artists to experiment with new sounds and styles.

In literature, generative AI is providing writers with tools to overcome creative blocks, generate new story ideas, and even co-write novels, short stories, or poetry. Models like GPT-4 and OpenAI's Codex are capable of generating coherent, contextually relevant text that mimics the writing style of renowned authors or adapts to specific genres. Writers can use these AI models to generate drafts, create dialogue, or explore alternative plotlines. In the case of advertising and marketing, AI tools can quickly generate compelling copy, advertisements, and social media posts tailored to specific target audiences, helping companies optimize their messaging and improve customer engagement.

One of the most transformative applications of generative AI in creative industries is in film and animation production. AI-generated visual effects, CGI, and even deepfake technology are revolutionizing how films are made. In animation, AI can generate lifelike characters, simulate realistic movements, and create expansive worlds based on minimal input from animators. Filmmakers are leveraging generative AI tools to speed up production processes, reduce costs, and enhance creativity by experimenting with novel visual styles and techniques that would otherwise require extensive manual labor and artistic expertise.

Generative AI is also democratizing creativity, making it accessible to a broader range of people. Tools that were once reserved for highly skilled professionals are now available to hobbyists, students, and emerging artists. With just a few prompts, anyone can create sophisticated digital artwork, music, or written content, breaking down barriers and making creative expression more inclusive. This shift is leading to the emergence of new forms of collaborative creativity, where human creators and AI work together in the production of art, fostering a symbiotic relationship that expands the boundaries of what is possible in the creative realm.

Despite the many opportunities generative AI offers, it also raises important questions about authorship, copyright, and the definition of creativity. If AI generates a piece of music, art, or literature, who owns the intellectual property? What rights do human artists have when AI is used to assist in the creative process? These are complex issues that will require ongoing debate and legal frameworks to address. Additionally, there are concerns about AI's potential to dilute the uniqueness of human creativity, with critics arguing that AI-generated content might lead to homogenized or repetitive outputs, lacking the deep emotional or cultural resonance that human creators bring to their work.

As generative AI continues to evolve, it is clear that its role in the creative industries will only grow more significant. AI is helping to shape the future of art, music, literature, and digital content, driving innovation, increasing efficiency, and enabling new forms of creative expression. The relationship between humans and machines in creative processes will continue to evolve, presenting exciting new possibilities and challenges for artists, creators, and consumers alike.

Generative AI in Business Strategy and Customer Experience

Generative AI is increasingly becoming a cornerstone in reshaping business strategies and enhancing customer experience across various industries. As companies seek to stay competitive in an increasingly digital landscape, they are turning to AI-driven solutions that not only streamline operations but also create more personalized, innovative, and efficient ways to engage with customers. By leveraging the power of generative models, businesses can not only optimize internal processes but also gain deeper insights into customer needs, preferences, and behaviors.

One of the key areas where generative AI is having a transformative impact is in the realm of customer experience (CX). Traditional methods of customer service, such as call centers and email support, often fall short when it comes to delivering fast, personalized, and consistent support. With the advent of AI, businesses are now able to provide 24/7 customer service through intelligent virtual assistants and chatbots. These AI systems are capable of understanding natural language, answering customer queries in real-time, and even handling complex transactions without human intervention.

Generative AI goes a step further by not only responding to customer inquiries but also predicting customer needs before they arise. By analyzing historical interactions, behavioral data, and context from previous communications, generative AI can generate tailored responses or suggestions that are highly relevant to each individual. This proactive approach helps build stronger relationships with customers, ensuring that their needs are met efficiently and effectively. For example, an AI-powered recommendation engine can suggest products or services based on past purchasing behavior, user preferences, or even external factors like seasonality or trending topics. These personalized recommendations drive engagement, increase sales, and improve customer satisfaction.

Beyond customer support, generative AI is revolutionizing marketing strategies. Traditional advertising and marketing campaigns often rely on generic messaging that targets broad audiences. However, with the help of AI, businesses can now create hyper-targeted campaigns that resonate with specific customer segments. Generative models can analyze consumer data and produce personalized content at scale, such as tailored advertisements, emails, and even product descriptions. This content can be adapted to reflect the interests, behaviors, and demographic characteristics of individual customers, leading to more effective marketing and higher conversion rates.

In addition to content creation, generative AI is being used to enhance the design and development of products and services. AI models can generate new product ideas, simulate design variations, and even forecast demand, helping businesses optimize their offerings and reduce the risks associated with product development. For example, in industries such as fashion or consumer electronics, generative AI can analyze current trends, consumer preferences, and competitor offerings to generate new designs or suggest features that are likely to appeal to customers. These insights can significantly shorten the product development cycle and reduce costs, while also ensuring that products align with customer demands.

Generative AI also plays a critical role in business intelligence and decision-making. Traditional analytics tools often provide historical insights that help businesses understand what has happened, but they fall short in offering actionable insights about what will happen next. Generative AI fills this gap by forecasting future trends, predicting market dynamics, and simulating various business scenarios. For example, businesses can use AI models to forecast sales, predict customer churn, or assess the financial impact of different strategies. These predictions allow organizations to make data-driven decisions with greater confidence, minimizing uncertainty and maximizing business outcomes.

Furthermore, AI-driven business intelligence tools can help identify previously unseen patterns and trends by analyzing large datasets, including unstructured data such as customer reviews, social media posts, and product feedback. By generating actionable insights from these diverse data sources, businesses can adapt their strategies to align with emerging market shifts, customer sentiments, and industry developments. In this way, generative AI supports the creation of more agile, responsive, and future-proof business strategies.

The application of generative AI in business strategy is not without challenges, particularly around ethics and data privacy. As businesses collect more and more personal data to fuel AI systems, they must ensure that this data is handled responsibly and in compliance with privacy regulations. The use of AI to predict customer behavior, for example, raises concerns about the potential for invasive surveillance and the need for clear consent processes. Additionally, AI-generated content, such as personalized recommendations or advertisements, must be transparent and avoid perpetuating harmful biases or stereotypes.

Despite these challenges, the potential benefits of generative AI for business strategy and customer experience are immense. As the technology continues to evolve, businesses that harness the power of AI will be better positioned to create innovative products and services, build stronger customer relationships, and make more informed decisions. With its ability to generate personalized, scalable solutions that address the unique needs of customers, generative AI is helping companies redefine what it means to deliver exceptional customer experiences in the digital age.

Chapter 8: From Buzzword to Business Value: A Roadmap forSuccess

Generative AI is no longer just a futuristic concept; it's a powerful tool with the potential to transform businesses. This chapter equips you with a roadmap to navigate the journey from initial hype to real-world business value.

8.1 Evaluating Generative AI Solutions: Selecting the Right Tool forthe Job

Not all generative AI solutions are created equal. Here's how tochoose the right tool for your specific needs:

- **Identifying Business Needs:** The first step is to clearly definethe business problem you're trying to solve. Is it streamlining content creation, optimizing product design, or personalizingcustomer experiences? Understanding your goals will guide your technology selection.

- **Understanding Different Generative AI Techniques:** As explored in previous chapters, there are various generative AI architectures (GANs, VAEs, etc.) Each has its strengths and weaknesses. Researching different techniques and their suitability for your specific task is crucial.

- **Evaluating Vendor Capabilities:** Numerous vendors offer generative AI solutions. Assess their expertise, track record, and the specific features and functionalities they offer. Look forsolutions that align with your technical infrastructure and data security requirements.

- **Proof of Concept and Pilot Programs:** Don't take a leap of faith.

Run pilot programs or proof-of-concept projects to test theeffectiveness of a generative AI solution in your specific context. This allows you to assess its impact and suitability before full-scale deployment.

By carefully evaluating your needs and available solutions, you can select the generative AI tool that unlocks the most significant value for your business.

8.2 Building a Generative AI Strategy: Integration, Implementation,and Change Management

Implementing generative AI isn't just about the technology; itrequires a strategic approach. Here are key considerations:

- **Integration with Existing Systems:** Generative AI solutions need to integrate seamlessly with your existing data infrastructure, workflows, and business intelligence tools. Planfor data exchange and ensure smooth information flow throughout the process.

- **Change Management and User Adoption:** Introducing new technology can be disruptive. Develop a change management plan to educate employees on how generative AI will impact their work and address any concerns. User training and supportare essential for successful adoption.

- **Scalability and Future-proofing:** Consider the scalability of yourchosen solution. Will it be able to handle growing data volumesand evolving business needs? Look for solutions with a clear roadmap for ongoing development and improvement.

Building a robust generative AI strategy requires careful planning, integration considerations, and a focus on user adoption. By addressing these aspects, you can ensure a smooth implementation and maximize the value of this technology for your business.

8.3 The Generative AI Journey: Continuous Learning, Adaptation,and Long-Term Value Creation

Generative AI is a rapidly evolving field. Here's how to stay ahead ofthe curve and ensure long-term success:

- **Continuous Learning and Monitoring:** Don't set it and forget it.

Continuously monitor the performance of your generative AI solution. Track key metrics, analyze outputs, and identify areas for improvement.

- **Data Feedback Loops:** Integrate feedback loops into your AI model. This allows the model to learn from user interactions and improve its outputs over time.

- **Embrace Experimentation:** Don't be afraid to experiment with different generative AI techniques and applications. This allows you to discover new use cases and unlock

unforeseen value foryour business.

- **Staying Informed:** The field of generative AI is

  constantly evolving. Stay up-to-date on the

  latest advancements, research,and ethical

  considerations to ensure responsible and

  effective use of this technology.

The journey with generative AI is an ongoing process

of learning, adaptation, and value creation. By

embracing continuous learning, experimentation,

and staying informed, you can ensure that

generative AI remains a powerful driver of

innovation and growth foryour business.